WILLIAM WALLACE
fReeÒom fíghteR

by

George Forbes

CONTENTS

Published by Lang Syne Publishers Ltd. Clydeway Centre,
45 Finnieston Street, Glasgow G3 8JU in 1996
and printed by Waterside Printers.
© Lang Syne Publishers Ltd, 1996.
I.S.B.N. 185 217 0182

INTRODUCTION

The figure of William Wallace towers above Scottish history just as his famous monument dominates from its rocky crag the flat pasturelands round Stirling.

He is a figure more of myth than of reality, a symbol as much as a historical fact.

His chainmailed legs bestride an era of Scottish history which transformed that nation from subservience into independence.

He was the catalyst, the inspiring force behind his countrymens' strivings.

He was the massive inspiration, the leader the lowly folk looked up to and he did not disappoint them.

Throughout his turbulent life, his name was like a fiery cross carried through the glens and his martyrdom, which was a political disaster on the part of his most vengeful foe, ensured his immortality in the hearts of Scots everywhere for succeeding generations.

And the amazing fact is that Wallace achieved all this with virtually nothing in his favour.

All he had was an almost superhuman strength, a dynamic, positive personality that would brook no opposition, a character armour plated with invulnerable convictions, a broad vision combined with the skill to strike fast and furiously, a mesmerising charisma that beguiled his followers and a determination that guaranteed victory even after death.

All of his feats were performed at a time when there were none of the instant communications of nowadays - no T.V. appearances, no newspaper interviews - yet he managed to stamp his personality on the people of Scotland with a firmness which led many to sacrifice everything for him.

There were two driving forces in his life - an inexhaustible belief in freedom for his countrymen and an undying hatred of English oppression which even led him to indulge in random murder.

Much of his career was savagery and butchery yet it was ennobled by his chivalric ideals and his long-term ambitions for Scotland.

His fame gained a new lease of life in 1995 with the release of the Mel Gibson Hollywood epic 'Braveheart', a critically acclaimed and popular recreation of the Scottish struggle for independence.

But even before that his figure loomed large in Victorian historical romances and he became the archetypal rebellious Scot. His phantom can be seen in the fictional figures of numerous Scots depicted over the years and his example has been taken as the norm of the defiant Caledonian freedom fighter struggling on against overwhelming odds.

Robert the Bruce may have been the eventual victor and the man who carried on to glory the standard first raised by Wallace but it is the latter who retains a warm affection in the hearts of his countrymen.

Bruce, despite his heroics and tenacity (both of

which were inspired by Wallace) nevertheless had a scheming, calculating politician's side to his nature, an ambitious instinct for seizing the main chance which was totally lacking in Wallace's more honest, humble sacrifices.

Wallace's straightforward love of his country has ensured he is always recalled with warm affection and there seems little likelihood of his prowess ever being ignored now.

Like King Arthur, that other once and future king believed to be just sleeping until he is really needed, Wallace is rediscovered by each new generation.

But he first sprang to prominence at a crucial point in Scotland's history...

CHAPTER ONE

A NATION ON THE BRINK

Scotland towards the end of the 13th century was in a state of turmoil as it struggled to assert its strength against its more powerful southern neighbour.

The Scots as a national, organised, cohesive force became a phenomenon in the hundred years prior to the peaceful reign of King Alexander 111 whose time on the throne was looked back on as a golden age.

The original Scots were the Gaelic tribes of the west who were of Irish descent.

The title of the nation did not indicate any close affinity of the other component tribes and clans - Picts, Britons and Angles - with the Gaels but came about because the fledgling nation accepted as their rightful ruler the man who had the inherited title implying feudal superiority - King of the Scots.

The powerhouses of this society were the abbeys and the castles that dotted the countryside, the one dealing with the spiritual aspirations of the nation and the other handling defence of the realm as well as daily law and order.

Castles could be huge, terrifying, intimidating, structures or humble keeps hardly more than a tower roughly made of stones. Walls could be 15 feet thick and 40 feet high. There was usually a metal portcullis and a wooden drawbridge and inside would be the equivalent of a small town with a buttery, a brewery, bakery, farmhouses, a falconry house, stables, armourers, servants and soldiers quarters, granaries, a wine cellar, a square courtyard, dungeons, a great feasting hall, bedrooms, kitchens, larders and pantries. Fireplaces were big enough to roast oxen. Lords and ladies slept on fragrant heather or thick straw, their rooms heated by roaring fires piled high with crackling logs, draughts muffled by intricate tapestries depicting chivalric romances lighted by wavering candles.

Abbeys and monasteries stood like islands of serene tranquillity in the brutal world marred by the clash of arms glinting in the sunlight and the death yells of the dead and wounded succumbing in the dust or the mud.

Religious leaders were taken from the ascetic ranks of the monastic orders and their rules were strict and unbending and their threats full of everlasting hellfire. Their beautifully designed buildings were ornate flowerings of the synthesised artistic and religious spirit that was the glory of the Middle Ages and their gardens were often rich in medicinal products as well as exotic, fragrant blooms. The monks established seats of learning and kept various arts alive, being expert in book illustration and teaching music.

The strictures of the Bible were taken very seriously indeed even by those who were not overtly attached to any religious institution. The powerful belief in scriptural fundamentalism led everyone to an everyday conviction that God and Satan were omnipresent and fighting each other, that the Christian teachings had to be obeyed at all costs and that the Church was the only bulwark against chaos and the forces of darkness.

Despite this deep and serious belief and faith in the Christian religion, it did not follow, given the fragility of human nature, that the medieval was any holier, when it came to sin, than any other age.

Trading burghs were the arteries of the growing mercantile and agricultural economy that was taking over from the old nomadic, pastoral clan system.

Small forts or fortified villages at road junctions or river estuaries became transformed into thriving towns.

Foreign trade was encouraged and the minting of a silver coinage encouraged Flemings, Normans and Danes to Scotland's shores.

King, abbot and baron drew rents from landowners, coins from tolls, taxes on wool, hide and cloth, flesh, fish and grain. The King's Chamberlain presided over the royal burghs, controlling them through sheriffs who were usually local lords.

In the towns, new guilds were formed, fraternal societies of craftsmen and tradesmen bonded together for mutual protection and advancement. Their centres were the guild halls or council chambers, usually in the middle of towns, and they had attained to a degree of independence from their feudal overlords which meant they were not likely to hand over their liberty to any invader rampaging up from the south.

The lower orders had been granted a glimpse of a prosperous future in which a man could improve his condition by the sweat of his brow and/or the use of his brains and upper mobility was becoming an increasing reality which they would now be loathe to surrender for a mud-caked serfdom.

The countryside was held together and ruled by a law and order which was the justice of the King and the barons, the Church and the burghs.

The King, who was believed to have a direct link with the Almighty, was the supreme arbiter in disputes and judgements and in his name two Justiciars rode throughout the land ensuring that his sheriffs were doing their work in proper civil and criminal administration.

Punishment was severe and exemplary. Usually this took the form of a straightforward public hanging for the most trivial of offences but there were also refinements like the pit, a black, airless hole below the castle's lowest dungeon. There were also various types of burnings and drownings and mutilations involving anything from torn tongues to broken ankles.

Life could be very basic, brutal and short and survival a daily priority, particularly through the long harsh winters.

However, the countryside was ever beautiful and rich in game and fish (including wild boar, wolves, deer, wildfowl, herring, eel, trout, salmon and sturgeon) and the people generally just wanted to get on with their lives and hopefully prosper and bequeath better living conditions to their offspring.

Each man was duty bound to defend his local lord's manor under the feudal system and thus, in an ascending scale, his king and country.

The Scottish soldier was by royal decree a mounted man, it being specified that everyone who possessed land or moveable property should keep at least one horse for use in public service. Though he fought on foot in battle, the Scot was invariably carried to the hostilities on his sturdy, shaggy horse bred in the Highlands by the Gaels and driven down to the marketplace of Berwick or Stirling.

The Scot on horseback could look rather quaint with his long legs, crude saddle, padded coat, iron hat, wooden shield and spear. These spearmen came into their own when they dismounted and formed disciplined schiltrons or hedgehogs of their bristling, vicious weaponry. These could prove formidable in attack and were difficult to break up, being able to withstand repeated cavalry charges.

The Scots were also adept with the claymore, a long, two-handed sword which could be slung over the shoulder on the march and unsheathed at the first sign of trouble.

The feudal obligation to bear arms and to be expert in their use was maintained by parades every six months during which every male between sixteen and sixty was expected to present their burnished weaponry for inspection.

Apart from spearmen, there were bowmen and mounted men-at-arms. Other popular weapons were daggers and axes.

The knights were invariably the lords of the manor and they were the equivalent of modern armoured tanks, rampaging decisively over battlefields but often proving unwieldy and difficult to manoeuvre, particularly in muddy conditions or where there were holes in the ground. Once unsaddled, knights were invariably cut down where they stood, deeming it dishonourable to surrender.

The knight was armed with a lance, a sword, an axe or mace and he covered his head with a steel cap and his body with glittering chainmail.

War harnesses on the horses were usually of light plate armour imported from Germany or Italy but only the wealthiest knights could boast such finery as they pranced over the battlefields.

The English armies had large entourages trailing behind them, wagons full of beef and wine, and, when they encamped, villages of colourful tents, with banners flying and shields shining, were spread out over verdant meadows. Camp followers included women, pages, courtiers, messengers, blacksmiths and armourers.

The Scots could not afford the luxury of huge siege engines but the English had plenty of these to laboriously haul along, most notably two wooden missile throwers nicknamed ominously War-Wolf and All-the-World.

. In addition, the English had a vast array of catapults and rock throwing equipment denied the Scots who were never good at siege operations but were more adept at hit-and-run tactics.

They were aided in this by the geography of the land, the soaring peaks and the chasms of the glens, the roaring rivers and the thick forests.

There was no urban sprawl or neat roads to tame the wilderness in those days and a guerrilla army could melt into the heather and continue a campaign of harassment indefinitely.

Even the main highways were little more than glorified tracks and an expert woodsman could track an invading army and choose his moment of attack.

The main battles were usually fought on the Lowland plains, most notably where the Highlands spectacularly swept down to the grassy pasturelands beside Stirling.

. This was Scotland's cockpit, a strategic area which

was central to controlling the main castles and lines of communication.

Occasions arose when the armies had to face each other in pitched battles for any outcome of a campaign to be suitably resolved, something which the leaders in charge always demanded and which national pride stipulated must be resolved at some point.

The English in theory had a superiority of arms and experience but it was they who were in hostile territory surrounded by a wily, brave, ruthless enemy who could choose how and when to begin hostilities.

In addition, they often had to rely on fleets offshore to keep themselves supplied over the long summer months, especially when the Scots embarked on scorched earth policies, denying the enemy any sustenance or material comforts.

Needless to say, this haphazard way of keeping an army on the march properly fed hardly ever went according to plan. Often storms would blow the ships off course or delay them while the Scots found it easy to ambush patrols and wagon trains or prevent the English from getting to suitable ports or harassing them if they ever got there.

Notwithstanding all these commando-style tactics, the Scots, often through a misplaced sense of honour, were sometimes drawn into battle against their long-term better interests when it would have been safer, if less dignified, to run away and fight another day.

But such was the code of chivalry in those days that when an enemy was sighted it was often felt that opponents were duty bound to clash and leave the outcome to the celestial court looking on from above.

Throughout the long campaigns which made up the period of struggle known as Scotland's War of

Independence, a saga partly instigated by William Wallace, the Scots always felt that they were in the right and that God was on their side.

They viewed themselves as the aggrieved party and the Scottish warriors were fighting for more than simply patriotic ideals - they were battling to defend their own hearth and home, their freedom and families.

By contrast, the English forces were, by and large, feudal conscripts or mercenaries recruited from other parts of the British Isles, like Wales and Ireland, and as such had no personal vested interest in the outcome of the struggle.

The knights who formed the elite fighting corps of the English army were obeying the orders of their feudal warlord and rode into the ranks of the Scots with the same elan and unfeeling brutality as they would against the French or any other faceless enemy at which they were pointed.

High morale and the optimism engendered by initial successes against a superior foe were a crucial factor in keeping the Scottish forces together whereas once panic set in with the English forces it was difficult to control and the men often longed to get back home by the quickest route possible.

Much of the forces arrayed on either side relied a lot more on intangible elements than mere metal and armour, strong horses and muscular arms.

These included the spirit of the men, their ideals and the power of their leaders and this is where a figure like Wallace came into his own.

Such was the background against which the drama of Scotland's struggle for independence was to be played.

The calamity which was to plunge the country into decades of bloodshed took place on the stormy night of

19th March, 1286.

King Alexander 111 had been feasting and drinking with his nobles in the hall of Edinburgh Castle and, despite the late hour, the wild night and the pleas of his attendants not to depart, the merry monarch defiantly declared he was going to spend the night with his attractive, young wife Ylonde at Kinghorn across the Forth.

The boatman at Queensferry grudgingly carried the King and some of his courtiers across the stormy waters of the Firth but, in the gale-whipped blackness on shore, Alexander became separated from his colleagues and his horse stumbled at a cliff face.

His body with a broken neck was found on the rocks below in the early morning daylight.

Alexander, whose reign was looked back on nostalgically as an era of peace and prosperity, had no sons and less than a year before his only daughter Margaret, Queen of Norway, had died in labour.

It was the baby daughter who had killed her who was now designated heir to the throne.

As she was obviously too young to reign, six Guardians were chosen to rule in her place until she was old enough, three of them north and three south of the Forth.

It was at this point that King Edward 1st of England, also known as 'Longshanks' and 'The Hammer of the Scots', entered the story.

He was proud, arrogant, fearless, ambitious, forceful, immensely strong and ruthless and he coveted the kingdom of Scotland as his own while holding its common folk as beneath contempt.

He had a great love for all things martial and his greatest delight was to sit, tall and commanding in the saddle, and view his knights galloping by in all their finery.

His approach to problems was blunt and brutal and this extended to politics and diplomacy, particularly with regard to his northern neighbours.

But his great strength was not simply physical.

He also had a shrewd military brain and was expert at moving his men swiftly and decisively when the occasion demanded.

Widely regarded as the best soldier in Europe, he took it as a constant personal affront that Scotland would never submit to him and much of his energies were spent in conquering that troubled land.

Hated by his enemies and feared by even those closest to him, he always liked to clothe his actions in the veneer of legal or religious justification and was not above terrorising lawyers and bishops into draughting pompous bogus documents explaining to the world the reason for his aggression and how it had been sanctified.

In reality, there was no justification for his invasion of Scotland.

Edward had fixed it in his mind, without consulting the Scots, that their country was in fact part of England but this was simply a disguised way of promoting the interests of the English against the Scots.

English plans for subjugating and exploiting Scotland have not survived but no doubt they existed in the minds of the administrators at least, if not in document form.

The eventual aim would no doubt have been to reduce Scotland to the status of a mere English colony, supervised by English garrisons and with an English Governor ensuring the interests of the south against the north.

Under such a scheme, Scotland would have been nothing better than a slave state which was something of which the natives were well aware and in the bitter fighting that lay ahead this gave them greater strength and a more inhuman ferocity.

However, with a - for once - peaceful conquest in view, Edward suggested to the King of Norway that the infant Margaret should marry his son thus uniting the two kingdoms.

But the English monarch's wily plans came to nought when the young girl died on the voyage to Scotland.

Her death now created a vacuum and no less than 13 claimants stepped forward and stated they were rightful heirs.

Edward supported John Balliol, grandson of the eldest daughter of David, Earl of Huntingdom, because of his English connection and his influence proved decisive.

As repayment for Edward's support, the day after Balliol's coronation the new monarch had to do homage to the Plantagenet as his lord, master and protector, a humiliating procedure which infuriated the Scots.

Balliol proved a timid puppet in Edward's hands and was easily influenced by his immediate entourage.

The English treated him with disdain and summoned him to London on flimsy pretexts often just to humiliate him.

But the patience of the Scottish nation snapped when Edward ordered Balliol to muster an army to help fight an English war against France.

Meeting at Scone in July, 1295, a Committee of Twelve - four bishops, four earls and four barons - easily persuaded Balliol to break from Edward and enter into alliance with Philip of France.

Balliol found a sudden reserve of courage and began the expulsion of English noblemen from Scotland while English merchants were openly murdered in Border towns.

Edward, his blood boiling, his fire up, came storming north with his crack troops, possibly now secretly delighted that he had an excuse to invade.

His army took Berwick then pressed on to Dunbar where the disorganised Scots were routed and after this the English had little trouble subduing the countryside.

They captured Edinburgh Castle after a ten day siege then came to Perth where a victory feast was held.

Realising that he had only the lukewarm support at best of many of his nobility, Balliol decided to submit once more to the English King.

In the churchyard of Stracathro in Kincardineshire Balliol appeared before the Bishop of Durham because Edward would not deign to put in an appearance.

Balliol wore only a shirt and drawers and in his right hand carried a white wand which he meekly gave to the Bishop as a sign that he handed over his kingdom to the English.

The disgraced monarch was then taken into captivity and after three years he was allowed to go to France with some gold and silver cups to pay his travelling expenses.

With Scotland now at their mercy, English troops rampaged through the countryside, hanging knights from roadside trees, raping women, burning houses, stealing cattle and taking even the knives from the tables.

The Stone of Destiny on which Scottish Kings were

traditionally crowned was taken south (although a persistent legend states that the monks of Scone hid the real stone, replacing it with one quarried nearby) and the Scottish nation's archives and regalia were stripped.

Edward departed with the declaration that he was glad to be rid of such filth.

He unwisely left behind the Earl of Surrey, John de Warenne, as Guardian of the Kingdom, a cantankerous, cold-hearted, old warrior who viewed the Scots as vermin and put his trust in the might of his sword.

Hugh de Cressingham, a churchman, was made Treasurer, a fat, lazy steward of Edward's wife who had just as little sympathy with his 'subjects' as the Guardian and who was obsessed with milking the Scots for as much coinage as they would surrender, being religious in title only. He too believed that if the Scots would not submit they should be treated to short, sharp lessons and were none the worse of a few good hangings.

Edward's brutal treatment of his northern neighbours and his obvious lack of subtlety or sophistication in dealing with them remained the fatal flaws in his character the rest of his life and they led onto a series of bloody revolts which a wiser, less bloodthirsty ruler could have avoided.

These uprisings the English had to spend much time and effort in subduing but they still ended in humiliation for the House of Plantagenet.

It was a policy which reaped a whirlwind of destruction and took no account of the growing sense of nationhood flowering in the Scottish nation.

Just as centuries later that other tyrant, Napoleon, callously paid no attention to the nationalism he was arousing in countries he was trying to trample under, so

A NATION ON THE BRINK

Edward seemed blithely unaware of the fires he was stoking up against himself and his country.

The other English knights and members of the ruling, occupation forces took their lead from Edward and their callous, belligerent attitude could only lead to trouble with a proud, ancient warlike race like the Scots.

The country was a restless tinderbox about to explode. All it needed was the spark, the fiery light to lead it from the depths of despair to hope.

That light suddenly appeared in the form of a fierce, fair-haired giant with piercing eyes, a scarred chin and muscular limbs who wielded his heavy metal claymore, often scarlet, as if it were a lethal toy.

His name was William Wallace.

CHAPTER TWO

PATRIOT GAMES

There are conflicting theories about the birthplace of William Wallace.

One version, generally held, was that he was the second son of Sir Malcolm Wallace who owned lands at Elderslie near Paisley in Renfrewshire and over the centuries that town has built a small, lucrative tourist industry round its main claim to fame.

However, a recent biographer, James Mackay, after extensive archival research claimed the real birthplace was Ellerslie, a small hamlet in Ayrshire.

It is unlikely that absolute conclusive proof will ever be forthcoming now and certainly the burghers of Elderslie, as one might expect, stick strictly to the traditional line.

So all that can be stated with any certainty is that he was born south west of Glasgow, the son of a small landowner, probably of Norman descent, or possibly Strathclyde British, around 1272.

PATRIOT GAMES

His family was not wealthy and he had none of the advantages of any ruling elite. He would have been taught the usual martial skills and apparently early on showed great dexterity with the sword and claymore, something which was to prove useful in the years ahead. He became an expert huntsman and was educated by clerics, retaining a deep religious sense despite the bloodshed in which he became embroiled.

Perhaps it was these priests who first instilled in him his intrinsic sense of freedom or perhaps it was just the exuberance of riding the green rolling pasturelands of the south west.

It was said he particularly liked the story of King David and knew the Jewish freedom fighter's psalms off by heart and they helped inspire him in his struggles for his nation.

Certainly, in common with other warriors of his time, William easily reconciled violence and piety in a medieval synthesis difficult for the modern mind to grasp.

In the 13th century might was usually deemed right but behind this crude simplification lay the theological argument that God gave strength to those that deserved it, that physical bravery was a virtue in itself and that courage was synonymous with leaps of faith.

Victors were said to have had the support of the angels while the vanquished were often dismissed as being too weak of character to triumph.

It was very much an Old Testament view of life with little room for the charity of the gospels.

Times were hard and produced hard men and any love in William's character was reserved for his immediate entourage and family although he was also imbued with a passionate patriotism for his country.

WILLIAM WALLACE FREEDOM FIGHTER

Even in the midst of his most violent campaigns he still found time to steal away to churches and take part in masses and he carried a psalter with him everywhere and consulted it piously on the eve of his greatest battles. It gave him comfort and inspiration and he was able to transfer this divine fire on to his followers.

This was the same kind of mentality which at this time led to the formation of warrior monks like the Templars and the Hospitallers who saw no contradiction in combining fighting skills with a deep Christian faith.

William grew into a huge figure for his or any other age, estimates putting his eventual height at six foot seven inches.

He was also extremely well built, muscular, strong and had terrific endurance and recuperative powers.

Since he had nothing going for him in the realms of wealth or aristocratic influence, these physical attributes proved vital in his struggles for supremacy against an enemy which was always more powerful than he or his followers.

Chroniclers described his eyes as diamond bright, said his face was evenly proportioned and that he was handsome and attractive with long, wavy, fair hair.

As he grew older he indulged in a luxurious beard, the normal attribute of martial men of the time.

When in a peaceful mood, he was said to be polite and decorous although with a tendency to solemnity and even sadness as if he had some private irreconcilable grief, a scar on his soul.

Despite this demeanour, he knew how to switch on the charm and had a lively sense of humour when the occasion arose and could crack a joke with his colleagues.

He was shrewd, compassionate to friends in need, generous with time and help when it was called for, kind to widows and orphans and with a veneration for the church and a respect for the clergy.

But there was another side to him when he was inflamed.

He detested treachery or betrayal and was ruthless in hunting out deceit and punishing it.

His justice was swift and rigorous to wrongdoers and when he lost his temper he could be a ferocious sight, even to those closest to him.

Fierce, intense, occasionally incandescent with rage, restless with nervous energy, full of vitality, William just needed a cause to channel his prodigious talents. It was not long in coming.

In many ways he was similar to his arch foe, Edward. Both were proud, hot tempered, warlike, passionate for their causes and ruthless in executing their martial plans.

But at the end of the day it was Edward who was the aggressor.

Under other circumstances, William could have lived his life peaceably at home but he was prodded beyond endurance by the depredations of the English to respond and in doing so led the way for his country.

Defiance seems to have run in the Wallace family for, when the nobility and landowners were ordered to personally swear an oath of fealty to Edward Plantagenet at the nearest town, the Wallaces were conspicuous by their absence.

Although neither wealthy nor aristocratic, Sir Malcolm Wallace was still obliged to take his oath at Ayr or Irvine, which were both garrisoned by English troops, or face the consequences.

When the latter descended on the Wallace household, they found Sir Malcolm and his eldest son, also called Malcolm, had fled to the Highlands while Lady Wallace, of whom we know virtually nothing, took her young son and hid with a friendly priest near Dundee.

Thus from an early age William had experience of being hounded by the English and expelled from his homelands.

There were sporadic revolts throughout the countryside at this time against English tyranny.

One of the more serious clashes took place at Loudoun Hill at the head of the Irvine Valley where Sir Malcolm was killed after a prolonged, bloody personal combat with an English knight in the midst of a fierce skirmish.

His eldest son was also severely injured and both these incidents, needless to say, deeply embittered William even further against the English.

Sometime around 1291 when William would have been approaching 20 years of age, the first reports of his active resistance surface.

It would not be difficult to imagine William's state of mind and his motivation.

The state of his country alone would have been reason enough for a headstrong, rebellious young man to take to arms against the English who had so arrogantly marched in.

But, in addition, the invaders had killed his father who had died fighting them, the Wallaces had lost their home, they were exiles, his elder brother had been badly injured and his mother was in mourning.

It was said that Wallace brooded on all these things but it would not have taken much time one feels for him to resolve on some kind of defiant action.

PATRIOT GAMES

At the very least, he had nothing to lose.

Below the walls of Dundee Castle became the scene of William's first close encounter with the hated English.

The keep had been handed over to a constable called Selby, a typically arrogant English usurper.

He had a son the same age as William who regularly swaggered through the town with various likeminded companions and on one occasion in December, 1291, he caught sight of William, not a difficult thing to do considering he towered over everyone else and was clad in a bright green outfit.

The Englishman made the fatal mistake of accosting William and haughtily demanded to know why a Scot should be so gaudily attired and ordering that he hand over the dagger which dangled from his belt since it was obviously too fine for the likes of him.

William angrily grabbed the Englishman, unsheathed the dirk in question and stabbed him through the heart.

The dying man's companions rushed to his aid and a couple of them went for Wallace but met the same fate as their friend.

As a crowd jostled round, William made good his escape down an alley and ran to the house of a relative where a housekeeper gave him a gown and set him down beside a spinning wheel. He was ignored by troops searching the houses.

When night fell, William escaped to his mother and they fled, disguised as pilgrims, to Dunfermline.

Eventually the pair made their way back to Ayrshire where they were told the news that William had now been declared an outlaw.

The hunted giant hid out with an uncle, Sir Richard Wallace, at Riccarton Castle but he became restless with confinement and one Spring day went fishing in the

River Irvine.

Unfortunately, a troop of English soldiers from the Ayr garrison happened to ride past and, in typical fashion, five of them detached themselves from the main body and galloped down to William, demanding he hand over the trout he had caught and which were piled at his feet.

William diplomatically offered them half but the soldiers demanded the lot and when the fisherman began to argue with them they swore at him, decrying his insolence and, drawing their swords, lunged at him.

William parried one blow with his fishing rod, striking a sword from a soldier's hand which he then seized, slicing at his attacker's neck, killing him.

His face flushed with fury, William hacked into a second attacker, killing him also, before cutting off the sword hand of a third.

Faced with this terrifying giant, the two others fled and William finished off the prone, wounded soldier.

William seized the horses and arms of the fallen and galloped off to tell his horrified uncle what had happened.

Having done this, he took to the forest where he gradually gathered the reputation of a kind of Robin Hood character.

He attracted a doughty band of loyal, like-minded brigands round his woodland standard and launched hit and run raids against English outposts and patrols, his courage and daring gaining him increasing fame.

Over the next few years the robbery and brigandage which the English attributed to Wallace became confused and intermingled with what the Scots regarded as guerrilla warfare against their oppressors.

What actually happened was a combination of both

but there seems little doubt that William's targets were always English and never his native countrymen although, from a mere robber's point of view, this too made sense since it was the invaders who were the wealthiest members of society at that time.

Probably William's attitude was that he was only robbing people who had stolen goods from his fellow Scots in the first place.

As the numbers supporting Wallace grew so did the variety of his tactics and the area of his operations.

He frequently took refuge in the huge Selkirk Forest whose dark mass spread over much of southern Scotland. This also proved a useful base for raids south.

Various stories are told of William's swashbuckling exploits during this period.

Being a hot-blooded young man, he had a passion for the ladies and often took desperate risks to have trysts with his chosen lovers.

His reputation made him attractive to many women and his physical attributes never disappointed them.

He often had to make moonlight escapes out of castle windows as men-at-arms clattered along corridors to ladies' bedchambers.

In disguise at fairs or marketplaces, he was often spotted and made hair-raising escapes, fighting off circles of enclosing troops with his double-handed long sword, a ferocious weapon which seemed light in his bloodstained hands as he swung it round his magnificent head.

He was expert at leaping onto horses' backs and galloping off, losing his pursuers in the hills.

Often he had the support of local townspeople and the country folk who would hide him or protect him from the hated English.

WILLIAM WALLACE FREEDOM FIGHTER

His adventures at this time inspired novelists like Jane Porter and Sir Walter Scott in the early 19th century who pioneered historical romances and their echoes can still be experienced in the swashbuckling films of Douglas Fairbanks and Errol Flynn.

Often these exploits would involve William coming to the aid of some harassed peasant being browbeaten or robbed by the arrogant English soldiery and this endeared him even further to his countrymen.

Of course, as is the case with such heroes, many of the incidents were embroidered and even made up in the constant retelling but what is certain is that there is a basis of fact to many of them and that William was indeed a lively, adventurous young man, inspiring to many but a thorn in the flesh of the English.

The transformation from woodland robber to leader of his country was a gradual one involving an accumulation of martial skills and a warlike reputation.

But the defining moment which finally made William realise that his destiny might be greater than merely being a pin-prick in the occupying forces occurred following one of the more serious incidents which involved a fracas in the streets of Ayr.

William was passing by when a servant was accosted by an English steward who demanded he hand over his bag of fish (the latter seemed to have had an ominous significance for William).

William told the steward to leave the servant alone and there was the usual argument with the Englishman lunging at the giant with his hunting staff and the Scot drawing out his lethal dagger.

But this time, as the steward collapsed dying from a stab wound, there were a large number of English troops with spears in the area who hedged William in and forced him towards the sea wall where he was over-powered, chained and plunged into the local dungeon.

William was put on a starvation diet, contracted a fever and went into a deep coma.

An examination apparently showed he was dead and the body was tossed onto a dungheap from where it was retrieved by an old nurse who used to work for the Wallace family.

As the body was being washed down for burial, the nurse noticed a faint flickering under the eyelids and realised William was still alive.

He was spoon-fed and her daughter, who had just given birth, breast-fed the prone giant and slowly he recovered.

However, to keep up the pretence of his death, a wake was arranged and a fake funeral.

When Thomas the Rhymer, the mystic poet of the Border country who was credited with second sight and various other magical attributes, heard that William had died he became alarmed and made further inquiries.

When reassured that the giant had in fact survived, Thomas predicted that the outlaw, before his own demise, would slay thousands of the English foe and eject them from Scotland.

This prediction had a profound effect. It reached the ears of William himself as he recuperated and gave him the feeling that his miraculous escape and recovery was a sign from Heaven that he was destined for greater things.

As the word spread throughout the countryside that Wallace had been 'resurrected' and declared to be the new Scottish leader everyone was looking for, the effect was electric on the populace.

And it set the alarm bells ringing among the English

who realised they now had in their midst not just some brigand of the hills but a focal point for all the various resentments that had been brewing since their arrival.

From now on, as he regained his prodigious strength, William was to emerge as a towering historical figure.

CHAPTER THREE

GATHERING STORM

From now on William took to constantly wearing armour of some kind and he ensured there was always a weapon to hand, whether his trusty dirk or his lethal claymore which he often carried on his back.

It was as if he realised he now needed to be constantly on the alert, vigilant against his enemies and ready to take advantage of every situation that came along.

If his views about the English had been grim before, they proved murderous now as he realised only the elimination and expulsion of his arch enemies would satisfy his destiny.

William found he did not need to start any revolt.

The seeds had long been sown by the brutal attitude of the invaders and rebellion was now truly in the air, particularly south of the old Wallace hunting grounds in Galloway where some of the local lords had been stirred into action by Bishop Wishart and James the Steward.

But it took the return of Wallace to galvanise the country.

He found the awakening ambitions of his country, stirred from their torpor by the arrogant, ruthless attitude of the English, now coincided with his own vision and aims.

He found himself strangely in tune with the times.

This was the moment when he could come to the fore and William seized every opportunity to place his name before his countrymen as a famed rebel while remaining a constant plague to the invaders.

After he had recovered from his brush with death, William set out on the road to Glasgow and en route had a bloody encounter with an English knight and two yeomen who tried to arrest him.

They ended up dead in the ditch for their troubles, the first of many.

Reunited with his uncle Richard at Riccarton Castle, William found himself reinforced with enthusiastic local young men as well as relatives from throughout the south west.

His first feat was the ambush of an English baggage train near Irvine which netted him horses, provisions, armour and money.

The English guards were slaughtered to a man and among the dead was the knight who had killed William's father.

William and his band hid in caves where they were joined by an increasing amount of headstrong or adventurous youths attracted by the magnetism of the Wallace personality and the glamour of what was already his legend.

The wily English tried on a couple of occasions to buy Wallace off, using intermediaries to arrange a tentative truce but negotiations with the headstrong giant were impossible and it was only a matter of time before any talks broke down due to the arrogance of the English and the powerful anger of the Scot who invariably ended up slicing to the ground his enemies, stealing their chattels and taking once more to the woods and the hills.

With sixty followers, William took the English outpost at Gargunnock Tower near Stirling, slaughtering the garrison, then the band went marauding throughout Perthshire, killing arbitrarily any Englishmen who crossed their paths.

On one occasion the Scots ambushed a band of ninety English soldiers near the Tay, charging forward with spears, disabling the horses, throwing the knights to the ground where their claymores chopped through armour, flesh and bone.

William was always in the thick of these frays and his volcanic power was capable of decapitating and severing limbs despite the heaviest armour.

To be at the receiving end of a personal Wallace onslaught meant certain death while the huge Scot himself seemed to walk through the carnage unscathed and undiminished in energy thus adding to his burgeoning reputation for ferocious invincibility.

Following the ambush by the Tay, the survivors were chased back to Perth Castle where William, far ahead of his men, held the drawbridge until they caught up after which the keep was burned down and every man inside put to the sword.

A thousand cavalry raced to the scene to entrap the outlaws who had retreated to a nearby wood.

The English also brought up 140 Lancashire longbowmen and showered William's position.

The Scot apparently had added archery to his other attributes and he possessed a strongbow which only he had the strength to use and he made each of his shots deadly accurate.

When he ran out of arrows, he darted forward and beheaded a few enemy archers.

Ferocious hand-to-hand fighting took place in thick woodland but the Scots were hopelessly outnumbered and had to retreat into the wild fastnesses as the sun set.

A few days later, William foolishly decided to visit one of his mistresses in Perth but he was recognised and pursued by the town guard.

Not for the first time he donned womens' clothing to make his escape out of the town gates but two watchmen became suspicious and pursued him, ending up stabbed to death while bloodhounds were put on William's trail and tracked him to Elcho Park.

More than 600 troops then charged into the Scots' position.

A fight to the death ensued with the Scots desperately battling for their survival, their backs to the River Tay before breaking through the English ranks and, led by Wallace, retreating towards the safety of moorlands in the gathering dusk, eventually escaping by swimming the icy Forth at Cambuskenneth.

William rallied his tired, depleted corps of followers and rode south to Bothwell Moor where the Christmas of 1296 was spent and where the Scots heard the news that the English believed Wallace once more to be dead.

Around this time William thought he would reassure his enemies in his own inimitable manner that he was alive and well so he made frequent visits into Lanark where he assassinated random Englishmen, usually by stabbing them or cutting their throats up dark alleys.

Since the county town was heavily garrisoned with English troops, the pickings were rich for a killer under the cover of the blackness of winter nights.

As if his life was not already complicated enough at this time, William fell in love with an 18-year-old girl, Marion Braidfute, who stayed in Lanark.

She was attractive, courteous, virtuous and humble and had good reason to hate the English who had killed her older brother.

William is reputed to have seen her first in the Church of St. Kentigern and had doubts as to whether he should pursue her even although she seemed to encourage him.

Feeling, correctly, that murder and love hardly fitted together and mindful that his last liaison in Perth had almost ended in disaster for his men and his ambitions, William was of the opinion that the courtship of Marion should wait until he had finally defeated the English and set Scotland free.

However, the attraction of the fair maid and the demands of his own virile flesh proved too strong for him and he frequently slipped into Lanark to see her.

She made sure he could gain easy access to her house and the affair seems to have been passionate and intense right under the noses of the English soldiers which no doubt gave added piquancy to their couplings.

They appear to have undergone some kind of wedding ceremony and there was talk of a daughter being born.

It is difficult to imagine what must have been going through William's mind on his nocturnal forays into Lanark during that winter when some of the time he would be cutting throats and hours later making love to Marion.

Whether she was aware of his murder raids is unknown.

Whether she would have disapproved, even if she had known, is problematical since she must have known of his reputation long before she allowed him into her midnight bedroom.

Like all his personal relationships with his supporters, William's charisma seems to have been enough to carry the day.

If he was as ferocious in his lovemaking as he was in fighting then he must have been a formidable bedmate indeed.

Once again word went round that the report of his death was untrue and again his reputation became greater.

He seemed unstoppable.

William went on a recruitment drive in Dumfries and Galloway and clashed with English cavalry near Lochmaben.

This proved so successful for the Scots (once more William had lopped off a few more heads) that it was decided to take Lochmaben Castle, a prestige proposal for what was still a ragbag band of brigands.

This was done using subterfuge - a local man managed to get the garrison to lower the drawbridge and William with a hand-picked party stormed across, slaying the guards.

For the first time the castle was not destroyed but held by William's men.

This was a significant step forward in Scottish tactics and showed they were beginning to form a strategy for expelling the English.

GATHERING STORM

William now returned to the environs of Lanark but on one of his frequent visits to the town he was spotted by some soldiers and was accosted in the street.

A ferocious fight ensued and at one point William sliced off an opponent's arm.

William and his companions, vastly outnumbered by reinforcements who kept arriving by the minute, managed to escape to Marion's house, leaving around 50 dead or wounded behind, and then out a back garden gate into the open countryside.

The English soldiers led by the Sheriff of Clydesdale, Sir William Heselrig, arrived outside Marion's house, demanding that she hand over Wallace but she defied them, barred the door and shouted at them from an upstairs window thus giving William time to make good his escape.

The soldiers smashed in the door but when Heselrig realised that William and his band had escaped he ordered Marion executed on the spot.

The girl was duly put to the sword at once, still yelling her hatred at the English soldiers.

When news of this reached William as he skulked in the hills he was prostrate with grief.

But not for long.

After dark, little groups of men began to wander back into the town.

The English troops, believing the Scottish outlaws were far away, paid them little attention, not even the large figure dressed like a monk.

But the groups met up in the marketplace and then headed off for designated houses.

William made straight for Heselrigg's house, burst in the door, ran upstairs and sliced through the Sheriff's skull as he lay cowering in his bed.

Houses were burned and wholesale slaughter ensued till the streets ran red with English blood.

Hundreds are believed to have been murdered by the vengeance-crazed Scots, only women and priests being spared as usual.

This single event, more than any of the forays, escapes and clashes which had preceded it, was like a bonfire signal to the rest of Scotland to revolt.

The massacre of an English garrison was an act of rebellion much more serious than roadside ambushes by a bunch of vagrant outlaws.

Everyone realised this, not least the English who made the capture of Wallace their number one priority.

It also showed that God did not appear to be on the side of the English since He had signally failed to protect them.

William Wallace was suddenly more than just a folk hero or a figure whose exploits were regaled round tavern firesides.

He had become a focal point for rebellion and many a young lord unsheathed his sword when he heard the news.

Wallace, heartbroken, exiled, outlawed, burning with anger, his powerful body exploding with rage, his sword hungry for blood, was ready to take on all the might that Edward could fling at him.

CHAPTER FOUR

BUILD UP TO BATTLE

William now found himself the leader of a small army as new recruits flocked to his standard throughout the Spring of 1297.

The whole of the south west, Wallace's home territory, was up in revolt and he could now call on at least three thousand well armed troops and many more hangers-on who simply needed to be properly trained and kitted out.

William led them northwards into the Highlands where Andrew de Moray, a young firebrand knight as audacious as Wallace himself, was raising mounted troops of Gaels whose flying columns struck terror into the hearts of the occupying forces, striking fast, hard and brutally before vanishing into the mountains.

A network of spies kept the Scots informed of English dispositions and various outposts and garrisons were attacked, especially in the north east, before the rebel army wheeled south and struck at the symbolic and administrative heart of English supremacy, over-running Scone where the English justiciar, William de Ormesby, was holding court and outlawing all those who would not submit to his king.

As the Scots stormed through Perthshire, de Ormesby leapt on his horse and galloped off to Edinburgh with his eye witness account of the revolt.

Surrey was down south attending to his estates and de Cressingham, fat, indolent and complacent, was in charge.

However, he was alarmed enough to take to the saddle, leading his troops out to subdue the revolt, but cautious enough not to take on Wallace.

Instead, he veered down to the south west where the local nobility had formed themselves into a rebellious confederation.

The English rightly considered these petty upstarts as easy targets and, after they had been surrounded at Irvine, the lukewarm rebels meekly surrendered, having no stomach for the fight.

Meanwhile, Wallace and his burgeoning army was storming across the northlands, taking most of the strongholds beyond the Tay, hanging the English from trees in mass executions.

His ally de Moray took Inverness and Castle Urquhart in the Great Glen and made a triumphal procession through Aberdeenshire.

The pair met at Perth and their followers cheered and flung their bonnets in the air and declared them the leaders of the army of the Kingdom of Scotland who fought for King John Balliol, declaring his abdication to be invalid and enacted under duress.

Always worried about finances, de Cressingham sent an urgent despatch to Surrey stating that not a penny in taxes had been raised for the treasury of which he was in charge and at long last the English army in the south stirred itself as Edward and his advisors realised the seriousness of the situation.

In the midsummer of 1297 conditions were chaotic north of the border with the horizon dotted with burning castles, no apparent law and order and nobody at all sure who was in charge of the country.

The English raised an army of 300 knights and 40,000 men-at-arms to subdue the rebellious Scots, a force which gave some of the nobility who had supported Wallace second thoughts.

To boost morale, William led an attack on Glasgow, galloping at the head of his men up the High Street. He ordered his followers to stock well the Clyde with English dead, a command which is commemorated in the name of Stockwell Street which leads down to the river. Clashes lasted several hours and the waters of the Clyde did indeed eventually flow red with English blood.

William then marched into Argyll, gathering support while the English forces concentrated in the Borders, building up their strength before taking on what they now realised would be a formidable foe. King Edward would dearly have loved to have led his troops northwards into battle but he was otherwise engaged fitting out another army for Flanders.

Throughout the summer William marched his men north eastwards taking every town and castle on his route, including Perth, until he reached Aberdeen where he fell on an English fleet in the harbour, burning the boats and plundering the cargoes.

Then he turned south once more and laid siege to Dundee which was tenaciously defended as was Stirling Castle.

In mid-August William was given the news that the English were at last on the move, marching up to relieve these two strongholds.

He determined to meet them on the green plain below Stirling Castle in one big, decisive battle, laid his plans accordingly and organised his forces to converge on the scene of what was to prove his greatest triumph.

CHAPTER FIVE

SHOWDOWN AT STIRLING BRIDGE

The English army which faced Wallace was the greatest fighting machine of its age.

It comprised the pride of English chivalry - proud knights bedecked in the finest armour, their huge warhorses with glinting harnesses champing at the bit, all bedecked in the colourful finery of heraldry with bannered lances, emblazoned shields and ornate helms - as well as Welsh, Gascon and Sherwood bowmen beside men-at-arms with spears massed like mobile forests.

The ranks were laced with veterans from campaigns in the Holy Land and France.

It was an army which had never known defeat, was full of confidence in the skills of its commanders and contemptuous of the Scots who had never fought the English on such a large scale before.

The Scots by contrast were a ragbag army, ill disciplined, poorly armed and with only a smattering of nobility to lead them.

It was drawn from the middle and lower orders, folk from Lothian and Galloway, Gaels from Badenoch and Moray, Picts from Fife, commanded by inexperienced knights and clan chiefs.

Some of their weapons were home-made like the long, twelve-foot spears as well as crude axes and knives.

Few of them had any armour and came down from the hills in their rough tunics, carrying their supplies of oats and lentils on bags over their shoulders, ready to take on the might of the invaders.

But they had Wallace - and for many that was enough.

For years they had suffered under the English yoke and for many, as for William himself, now was the time to strike back decisively and free their country once and for all.

Morale was surprisingly high for they realised they could do great things on the rolling grasslands below Abbey Craig on which they took up their positions above the gaudy banners of their enemies.

By contrast, the English army was a feudal host made up of conscripts obliged to serve their masters and lay down their lives if necessary for the Crown.

The crucial focal point of the battle which was about to unfold centred on a wooden bridge over the River Forth which meandered, slow, deep and wide, between the jagged outcrop of Abbey Craig and Stirling Castle.

On September 10th Surrey, in overall charge of the English forces, sent an envoy to the Scots demanding their submission.

William told the messengers, "Tell your people we have not come here to gain peace but for battle to avenge and deliver our country. Let them come up when they like and they will find us ready to meet them to their beards."

He ordered his spearmen to hold their ground until they heard his horn, which only he was allowed to blow, and then to charge forward downhill.

That evening Surrey gave orders that his men should be prepared to cross the bridge early the following morning, despite the fact that such a hazardous frontal attack was unnecessary.

The wooden structure was so narrow that only two horses could comfortably ride over it abreast whereas there was a ford further down the river where fifty horsemen could pass over in line.

However, at this crucial juncture de Cressingham, with his mean spirit and penny pinching ways, chipped in with the comment that Edward's money should not be wasted any further on this war and that the bridge should be the means of attacking the Scots as quickly as possible.

At dawn five thousand English foot soldiers duly crossed the bridge but Surrey, exhausted from his trip north, was still asleep so the men-at-arms, lacking any orders, turned around and recrossed the Forth back to camp.

Eventually, Surrey bestirred himself, held a parade and conferred knighthood on some youths (as was the custom before a big battle), some of whom were only to live to enjoy this honour a few hours.

Surrey, gazing out at the Scottish spears glinting in the distance like the quills of a huge hedgehog, was given conflicting counsel.

An old soldier, Sir Richard Lundin, who had deserted from the Scottish ranks, pointed out to him the hazards of a slow crossing of the bridge with a prepared enemy on the other side but de Cressingham was impatient as ever and, although he had no military experience, gave the opinion that further delay would be intolerable for the prestige and honour of English arms.

Surrey, in an indolent, dithering manner, listened to the corpulent priest-treasurer and gave the order to cross over the bridge at once with de Cressingham leading the way.

Slowly, the cumbersome English army began to make its way over the wooden structure throughout the morning.

The younger elements in the invading army were restless and keen to get across as fast as possible so that they could take on these upstart Scots and they fanned out once they had crossed the rickety wooden structure, their gaudy banners blowing in the late summer sunshine.

Half a mile away, William, viewing the slow movements of the English forces from his high vantage point, kept his troops standing in line and held his hand patiently.

Their forbearance must have been great as they saw the ranks of their enemies swell below them and William must have stayed calm as he came under pressure to launch an attack.

But he knew a premature move would prove inconclusive while to wait too long would give the numerical advantage to his foes.

The English knights, mistakenly viewing this inaction as cowardice, were now keen to charge, even although only half of their men had crossed over the river.

Suddenly, before the English could properly deploy for a charge, William, judging that enough of the enemy were spread below him to be decisively defeated, gave a mighty blast on his horn and the Scots surged down from the heights, yelling their bloodcurdling war cries and hacking their scarlet, screaming way towards the bridge which they were desperate to secure, their momentum carrying them into the enemy ranks.

Men were trapped on the wooden structure, pushed by those pressing forward from behind but crushed back by the retreating troops.

Panic stricken, many dived into the river where they drowned, pulled down by their sodden equipment and armour.

Bowmen, unable to use their weapons, were cut down where they stood.

William had secretly sent a small band of men down to the end of the bridge where the supports had been weakened.

They quickly smashed through the wood, sending the bridge plunging into the river, drowning more of the enemy and trapping those who had already crossed.

Knights tried to fight their way out of the enclosing noose but spears hemmed them in, dirks slit their throats under their helmets after they had fallen from their terrified, hamstrung horses and the Scots charged over them, yelling and screaming, their claymores and battle axes swirling, smashing into them, cutting and slashing with their ferocious weapons, soaking the green grass with red English blood.

De Cressingham, sweating and desperate in the vanguard, was pulled from his saddle and put to the sword.

His body was later skinned, pieces being torn off as trophies of vengeance. William used some of the flayed flesh as a baldrick for his sword and it was also used as saddle-girths for his horsemen. Other parts were displayed around the countryside in triumph.

The English forces were now effectively cut in two

but for an hour Surrey on the other shore could only watch as his troops were butchered and flung in the river, as metal glinted in the sunlight and the clamour and agonised screams of battle wafted in his direction.

No prisoners were taken as the trapped forces were methodically hacked to pieces, few of them managing to scramble to the other side of the river.

Estimates of the English dead have been put at more than four hundred knights and archers and five thousand footsoldiers. The bodies were piled up at the foot of Abbey Craig.

Scottish losses were negligible but de Moray died from terrible wounds, the one heartbreak of the day for William.

Surrey turned and fled from the nightmare carnage, spurring his horse at a gallop all the way to Berwick, abandoning his army and the garrisons at Stirling and Dundee to the tender mercies of the Scots.

For days afterwards the retreating English troops were harried by William and his army, their baggage trains looted and stragglers massacred.

A brutal clash took place at Haddington, resulting in a further slaughter of the invaders and by the time the tattered remnants of the English forces reached the Tweed it has been estimated that they had lost a total of ten thousand men.

It had been a comprehensive victory on the part of William and his followers against vastly superior odds and it placed him firmly in control of the country.

There was much celebrating throughout the countryside and many a ceilidh lasted for days in the mountains and the glens as the victors drank heavily, danced and sang and split up the spoils among themselves.

It had shown the Scots that through guile and proper

leadership they could fling off the belligerent advances of their southern neighbour and it was a bloodstained signal to Edward that he could not take the subjugation of the north for granted.

The nationhood of Scotland was forged with metal and blood at Stirling Bridge and there could be no turning back now for William and his followers.

For the English it was an ignominious and demoralising defeat which destroyed once and for all their aura of invincibility.

William was now free to bring into being the nationhood of Scotland but he realised time was short.

Edward would once more be casting his eyes northwards, seeking vengeance.

The Scots knew they had struck a blow against English ambitions but had not mortally wounded them.

CHAPTER SIX

OVER THE BORDER

The Scots, exhilarated from victory, did not stop at the border, not when Cumberland and Northumberland lay at their mercy and not with the memories of English depredations fresh in their minds.

So they crossed over and galloped their shaggy ponies over the northern English shires, pillaging and killing and burning towns, villages and farms.

William found it difficult to restrain them since he had no treasury with which to pay them and the men felt they were deserving of all the booty they could lay their eager hands on.

It was said that for a month the worship of God stopped in every monastery between Newcastle and Carlisle and only William's intervention stopped monks being slaughtered at their altars.

He strongly disapproved of the murder of civilians and the desecration of churches and told the priests of Hexham, "Remain with me for I cannot protect you from my soldiers when you are out of my presence!"

The Scots had no siege equipment so could not take any castles and the gates of Carlisle were closed against them but there was no real resistance against their ravaging bands.

Meanwhile, William wrote to the merchants of Hamburg and Lubeck inviting them to resume trade with Scotland "because our country, thanks be to God, has been recovered by war from the power of the English."

William's priority, as he tried to bring some semblance of order to the country he had freed from foreign domination, was to resume normal, commercial operations with as many nearby nations as possible so that he would be in a strong position to resist the might of the English which was bound to be launched against him at some point in the future.

There was famine in many parts of Scotland due to a poor harvest that autumn and this led to the systematic stripping of Cumbria by William's army.

They carried off everything they thought might be useful to them and what was left behind was put to the torch.

Anyone who resisted was summarily executed.

A flying column went further south to invade County Durham but they were stopped by a severe blizzard in November and the Scots wisely decided it would be more prudent to turn back for home.

If it had not been for the bad weather they could have pressed on because there was no serious force to stop them.

The Bishop of Durham of course saw the hand of God interceding in the snow but the Scots had overextended their lines and could have done little more without reinforcements.

Exhaustion now set in amongst the invaders who found themselves with little left to carry off in the wasted countryside.

Most of the Scottish army had retreated back over the border by December but it had proved a lucrative follow-up for them to the battle of Stirling Bridge.

The destruction and damage perpetrated by the Scots had been savage and ruthless, lacking any sense of chivalry or morality, but it was no worse than what the English had committed north of the border.

And it could be said that the Scots had a semblance of right on their side since it was the more powerful English who had tried to conquer Scotland in the first place thus unleashing the torrent of bloodshed.

Such methods cannot be judged by any kind of modern Geneva Conventions.

In those days it was often a case of survival of the fittest and kill or be killed.

CHAPTER SEVEN

GUARDIAN

William had always been a big man but now his figure bestrides the annals of history.

The detailed facts of his life are often elusive and sometimes he darts in and out of events like a will o' the wisp before bursting onto the scene with explosive, conclusive force.

But now he took on the dimensions of a towering figure central in the development of his country.

For many he was like an answer to a prayer and he symbolised a sense of nationhood which had been simmering for years and which had actually been strengthened by the clumsy, unfeeling intervention of the English under their brutal and blundering king.

As a recognition of victory, William was knighted and appointed Guardian of the Kingdom of Scotland and Leader of its armies "in the name of the illustrious Prince, Lord John, by the Grace of God King of Scotland, by consent of the Community of that Kingdom" according to a charter drawn up at a ceremony in Perth.

Many of the nobility, who had sworn allegiance to Edward or had changed sides on at least one occasion, now found themselves in an awkward position.

They had a snobbish disregard for William, unwilling to serve under someone who was only a small, landed laird and who styled himself a representative of the people.

These knights, barons and earls, who were supposed to lead the common folk and show a good example, were a treacherous bunch at the best of times and William had his hands full trying to keep up with their intrigues while staying on the look-out, trying to anticipate Edward's plans.

One of the few people who had never taken an oath of fealty to anyone and therefore could not be accused of double dealing was William himself.

There were also competing claimants to the throne like the Comyns and the Bruces who, while they might sympathise with William's aims for his country, could have no support for anyone who recognised John Balliol as the rightful ruler.

In addition, some of the knights were simply jealous of William's achievements, secretly believing he made many of them look small in more ways than one.

For the moment William was lucky that Edward was still fighting in France and the barons he had left behind, still smarting from their defeat at Stirling Bridge, were disorganised and had no strategy for dealing with the upstart north of the border.

The best they could manage was the relief of Berwick Castle which had been under siege for months and a brief foray as far as Kelso before retreating quickly back south to the safety of Newcastle.

Simply by the force of his personality, William brought his nobility to heel so that, when summoned to a conclave in York by the English aristocracy, they refused to attend.

Just as he had been ruthless in warfare, William was now efficient in running his new kingdom.

During the first few months of 1297 William organised the countryside into military districts and raised fresh levies of troops to defend the southern marches.

Gallows were erected where suitable to threaten those dithering about conscription and William is said to have paid a sudden visit to Aberdeen and hanged a few young men, "to encourage the others" no doubt.

In addition, foot soldiers were rigorously trained in close order drill, most notably in forming the schiltron which was a compact grouping of spearmen with twelve foot long weapons bristling in every direction, a formidable obstacle to cavalry.

Ahead of his time, William also introduced a meritocracy, appointing lowly born people to high positions, rewarding those who, like himself, had sacrificed much for their nation.

This went against the elitist ethos of feudalism but seemed more in sympathy with the Celtic character and its tradition of mutual aid in need which did not clash with a respect for successful individuality.

However, this egalitarian innovation was another cause for grumbling among the nobility who saw their whole way of life under threat.

William's increasing base of support was the common folk but his views tended to alienate the aristocracy who were petty, selfish and hell-bent on defending their pampered way of life, even at the expense of the country's liberty.

Many of them felt it was better to live under a totalitarian like Edward than an egalitarian like William.

In an age when ecclesiastic controversies had a prominence over more mundane matters, William also purged his country's churches of English clergymen and monks.

Some of them were no doubt physically ejected by those eager to be rid of them but the later claim that some were murdered seems unlikely, even allowing for the bitterness of the times.

The Scots had held out a faint hope that they might get some material support from France but this was dashed when Longshanks made a truce with Philip in Gascony and returned home to deal with his recalcitrant northern neighbours, still viewing Wallace as nothing more than a glorified brigand.

Philip, devious and cunning, would have proved a dubious ally at the best of times and the Scots found themselves isolated with other countries having been intimidated by the might of England and its military prowess.

But north of the border people realised that they could look after their own affairs and prosper.

They realised under the benign rule of their Guardian the true meaning of liberty and they looked back on their sufferings under the English invaders with even greater bitterness and were determined not to revert to that subservient state.

Meanwhile, Edward moved the seat of his government to York, so that he could run his realm while supervising the conquest of the Scots, and in July crossed the Tweed at Coldstream with twelve thousand five hundred foot soldiers and two thousand cavalry, veterans of campaigns in France and Wales.

Erect in his burnished saddle, towering over his dusty troops on his black war horse, Edward, his blond hair turning white, was determined to wreak havoc on the Scots and bring Wallace to heel once and for all.

They slowly moved north by Roxburgh and Lauderdale, circling round Edinburgh and fanning out onto the Stirling plain, demolishing any outpost in their path.

However, the English did not have it all their own way.

Their long, drawn-out lines were vulnerable to the hit and run tactics so beloved of William's cavalry and stragglers were swiftly despatched.

In addition, campfires at night were not enough to illuminate Scottish assassins lurking in the dark, all of which had a demoralising effect on the army.

But, what was much worse, the English troops were hungry.

In fact, they were starving.

The fleet that should have provisioned them up the east coast had been delayed by unseasonal stormy weather.

Disease in the ghastly, haunting shape of the plague also stalked their ranks.

All of which caused rumblings of discontent and even threats of mutiny and Edward, as he approached Linlithgow, toyed with the idea of falling back on Edinburgh where he might calm and feed his restless followers.

Then the news he had been awaiting from his scouts out scouring the countryside finally reached him - the Scots army had gathered in the great forest by Falkirk.

Edward thanked God then marched as fast as possible to meet Wallace and, he hoped, recover the honour and glory of English arms.

By covering much ground overnight he stood within striking distance of the Scottish position and, although he did not know it at the time, by this tactic alone Edward had also secured his desperately needed victory.

He knew the next forty eight hours were crucial and that his army must be given the taste of victory or it would collapse from fatigue and disillusionment.

He also knew the way the Scottish mind worked when it came to martial manoeuvrings and he correctly foresaw that they would dodge around, relying on his cautious withdrawal to the capital to save face, whereas he was determined to catch the Scots on the hop and nail them into defeat.

It was his tactical decisions which were now to prove vital to the future career of William Wallace.

CHAPTER EIGHT

NEMESIS AT FALKIRK

William had withdrawn much of the population from Berwickshire and the Lothians once the English invasion had begun and his scorched earth policy had added to the acute discomfort of Edward's army.

The Scottish forces comprised mainly the peasantry, the working classes of the towns and the lesser nobility, all bound together in the holy cause of defending their nation against tyranny.

The Scots, however, had no natural barriers like rivers or rocks which they could utilise in their position near Falkirk and so faced their enemies with a degree of fatalism, putting the outcome in God's hands.

The Scottish commanders were in disagreement about the tactics to be used against the enemy but there was a general feeling that the English must be stopped in their tracks once and for all in the Lowlands and taught a lesson that would reinforce that of Stirling Bridge - that the Scots were not a nation to be trampled underfoot.

There was a false optimism in the Scottish ranks engendered by the memory of their stirring victory at Stirling Bridge but they failed to realise the calibre of the King they now faced.

Wiser heads among the Scottish ranks pointed out that the English seemed to be weakening daily and that it would be foolish to rush into battle with them when they could safely be picked off at a more leisurely pace.

But the old ethos of the chivalric ideal returned to haunt the knightly ranks of the Scots and it was felt by many that honour decreed the invaders be squarely faced down on Scotland's hallowed soil.

Meanwhile, unknown to their enemies, there was drunken dissension in the English ranks.

Edward had dispensed wine on the eve of battle in the hope that this would pacify his troops but the ploy backfired when they started squabbling among themselves and the Welsh recruits indulged in fisticuffs with their English comrades.

It took strenuous efforts to stop full-scale rioting from breaking out.

In addition, Edward, who, after pacifying his belligerent troops, had been lying, exhausted and sleeping, on the ground, was suddenly trampled by his horse picketed beside him, sustaining two broken ribs in the darkness.

A rumour swept the camp that the king had been killed so Edward deemed it prudent, despite his severe pain, to mount his saddle and exhort his troops to battle in the chill, before-dawn gloom.

After all the travails of the past few weeks, the sight of their King, towering, erect, defying his agonies and fierce on horseback, over them and telling them that the moment they had all been waiting for had come at last, proved inspiring and showed the psychological insight Edward had into the morale of his army.

The men moved out swiftly, glad to be active, and soon spotted the Scots deployed a mile away on a hillside.

William's army seems to have been surprised by the speed of the English advance which had taken place before sunrise when they had not expected any movement on the part of their enemy and it seems likely that the Scots had become complacent over repeated reports from spies and scouts that the English were in disarray and assumed the troubled invaders would therefore be falling back on Edinburgh for supplies.

What the Scots did not realise was that Edward was much more interested in spilling their blood than in filling the bellies of his troops.

He exhorted his men to tighten their belts, promised them Scottish booty before sunset and urged them on to death or glory.

With this swift approach of the vastly superior English forces, it became immediately obvious that any retreat on the part of the Scots would prove disastrous and turn into a rout over the flat Lowland plains, especially with the massive English cavalry able to harass them.

Therefore, although outnumbered two-to-one, the Scots decided to stand and fight.

The dynamism of the English forces which had proved so decisive even before battle was joined was due to the powerful personality of Edward and William now appreciated, too late, that this was no weak, fat or lazy leader.

The Scots really had a fight on their hands against a

truly formidable foe and would need not just all the brawn they could muster but also a lot of brains on the part of their leaders.

But the lay of the land left William and his commanders little room for manoeuvre, especially since time had run out for them and the advantage seemed to lie to some extent with the enemy.

Perhaps this was the reason that William's harangue to his men was less than inspired.

He told his spearmen, "I have brought you to the ring - dance if you can!"

Standing behind a flimsy barrier of stakes and ropes and a strip of bogland that would delay but not stop a charge, the schiltrons braced themselves, front ranks kneeling and inner ranks standing, their long weapons glinting in the sunshine, ready to withstand the inevitable cavalry charges that must come their way.

Between four of these schiltrons William positioned his Selkirk bowmen and on the flanks were the makeshift cavalry, a small force under Sir John Comyn more suitable for boosting morale than inflicting injury.

In agony from his shattered ribs, Edward allowed his judgement to be won over by his eager young knights, keen to get at the enemy.

He pulled himself onto his charger and shouted, "On then, in God's name - and may the day be ours!"

An English column comprising glittering knights led by the Earls of Hereford and Lincoln charged forward but became bogged down almost right away in the deceptively grassy looking stretch of marshland which they had not seen.

As they floundered to extricate themselves, the cursing knights could hear the jeers of the Scots.

A second English line led by the Bishop of Durham

then cantered forward, veering off diagonally to avoid the swamp, where the first line still struggled almost comically in the mud, and outflanking the Scottish left wing.

A third line commanded by Edward himself came up in support and the knights, under the stern gaze of their suffering sovereign, bravely charged the schiltrons while the first line, now finally free of the bog, wheeled round in a disorderly attack on the Scottish right.

Pressed on every side, with arrows showering down on them, the shiltrons displayed the result of months of training and, with commendable discipline, held firm.

But slingers using rocks accurately cut swathes in the Scottish ranks and the Red Comyns' inexperienced horsemen took fright when they saw the huge, neighing beasts of their brightly caparisoned English opponents bearing down on them, the horses' nostrils flaring and panting mist in the air and the sunlight glinting off ferocious weaponry, and a general panic ensued in their ranks which their leader was unable to control. It became a case of gallop off or be slaughtered.

William and his immediate staff were now the only horsemen left and they galloped up and down, exhorting the spearmen to hold firm.

The Scottish archers were swept aside by the English cavalry and the English bowmen with their superior weapons took an increasing toll of their enemies.

Edward now committed his infantry to the fight and stout men-at-arms hacked and chopped their way through the Scottish ranks and by sheer weight of numbers began to punch gaps in the schiltrons thus allowing the cavalry to pour through, creating havoc.

Once this happened, the Scottish forces were split asunder and they were cut down in crimson swathes.

The Bishop of Durham, meanwhile, had led his men round to the rear and charged uphill into the fleeing Scots, massacring all of the enemy who came within the deadly range of their scything swords and axes.

For the English infantry it became a case of routine, slogging butchery, slashing and hacking their way through the broken wooden spears and prone bodies of their opponents, wading up to their knees in blood and slipping on the bodies piling up in front of them which they had to clamber over.

William, with a small bodyguard, managed to gallop to safety across the bloodstained grass to the shelter of a nearby wood and from there he retreated to Stirling, setting it ablaze before retiring into the hills.

The infantry he had left behind continued to be killed in their thousands and no quarter was given as the bodies continued to mount up and the English yelled at each other to remember Stirling Bridge.

The slaughter only ended as dusk fell and in the fiery sunset the field of battle was bathed in a gory glow.

For the moment Scotland's dreams of freedom had perished with her army.

On reflection it was a grave mistake for William to have faced the English in this pitched battle.

He should have stood back and allowed the English forces to dissipate their energies throughout the barren Lowlands before hitting them with the guerrilla tactics at which the Scots were so expert.

Edward's army was on the point of collapse when the Scots were spotted by their scouts.

The invaders were hungry, mutinous, diseased and fighting amongst themselves and would not have lasted many more weeks in such a hostile environment.

The Welsh levies would probably have deserted, the

lines of communications could have been severed or disrupted and, as summer gave way to winter, they could have been picked off at leisure by the Scots.

All of that was flung away by the battle of Falkirk.

What seems to have put William off balance was the sudden night march towards his forces of the English which made retreat a hazardous operation, thus forcing a showdown.

The credit for that must therefore go to the energy and initiative of 58-year-old Longshanks himself, even if his motivation was forced on him by the restive nature of his army which had to have a quick victory or it would have disintegrated.

Such was the prestige of William that it was believed that the Scottish nobility and in particular Robert the Bruce must have betrayed him at Falkirk for him to have so signally failed.

In fact, the Scottish barons did not let him down and Bruce had nothing to do with the defeat. The Comyn had fought with his customary valour and had only been let down by a sudden panic among the ranks of his inexperienced colleagues.

William had been let down by his own lack of campaigning experience and he had been simply outgeneralled by a superior foe.

But, even so, it was a Pyrrhic victory for the English although they had averted disaster.

They found Stirling a burning ruin and the country around laid waste and, still hungry and angry, they responded by burning St. Andrews.

They then fell back on Edinburgh to resupply, which is what the Scots had mistakenly expected them to do all along, and Edward bitterly returned south for the winter, promising his beleaguered governors in the lonely outposts of their castles that rose like islands round the blackened countryside, that he would return in the Spring "to punish the Scots and put down their disobedience and malice."

It took him three long, disruptive years to fulfil his harsh promise and, meantime, daily life proved extremely hazardous for any Englishman north of the Tweed unless he was safely ensconced behind thick masonry or surrounded by bodyguards.

But one thing the English had done was smash the prestige of William Wallace and his reputation for invincibility.

His eight months of governance were over even if they were never forgotten.

He had given his countrymen a taste of nationhood and independence and it was a heady brew which would not leave their psyche until they had finally cast off the English yoke.

As he galloped north to Callendar and the safety of the Highlands, William must have bitterly realised that with the loss of so many dear comrades a turning point had occurred in his life, even if he was thankfully unaware how steep the decline would be from now on.

He had come back from the dead at least once before but to repeat the trick would prove more problematic in the future.

CHAPTER NINE

THE STAG AT EVE

Many historians more or less write off the seven years between his defeat at Falkirk and his final execution as a blank period in William's life when in fact he was extremely busy doing what he was best at - harassing the English at every opportunity.

However, some of the blazing, vibrant spirit seems to have gone out of him, hardly surprising under the circumstances.

He gave up the official guardianship of his country, having no choice in the matter since he now had no army to back him.

His leadership had faltered at a crucial moment and his military judgement had proved fatally flawed. He had been caught wrong-footed by a shrewd, experienced campaigner, more adept at coping with that vital moment, which can win or lose a battle, than he, and, although there was no shame in one defeat, it had exposed starkly the shortcomings of the Scots.

In addition, William had lost many close friends to English blades and arrows and this plagued a conscience which, under other circumstances, saw nothing wrong in decimating the enemy.

What was worse, God had obviously turned his back on him and the destiny of William Wallace was not as clear-cut as had previously been indicated by the once fortuitous turn of events.

His followers, those still free, alive and unwounded, were demoralised and he was now seeking a fresh role to fit in with his drastically changed circumstances.

From being the leader and inspirer of his nation, he was now a hunted outlaw, foraging as best as he could in the forests and hills, raiding down on the English whenever he could, relying on secret supporters for sustenance.

But his example had aroused the ambitions of others and, although he had seemingly failed, the fact that he had been so successful for so long against superior odds caused certain members of the nobility to ponder whether they should continue to submit to foreign rule.

There was also a general feeling around that if William had avoided battle at Falkirk the much vaunted English forces would have been worn down by attrition, disease and hunger and sent packing off south once more.

An opportunity had been missed but that was not to say another might not arise to get rid of Longshanks' tyranny.

The ageing, aggressive Plantagenet could not go on indefinitely.

Already he was ancient by medieval standards, when most people were dead by forty.

In addition, he had suffered numerous wounds over

the years and had undergone long spells of hard campaigning in all weathers and, although he had many elements of the superhuman about him, he was at the end of the day merely mortal.

His major flaw when it came to his Scottish subjects was a total lack of sympathy or subtle diplomacy.

He took the crude view that brutality was the only thing the Scots understood and in this he was wrong.

It was a counterproductive policy which merely stoked up hatred against the English.

What was also well known to Scottish rebels was that Edward's son was weak and immoral and had none of the driving military genius of his father.

Many of the Scottish barons believed that once Longshanks was in his grave an opportunity for a more realistic revolt against a less ferocious enemy would present itself, a shrewd judgement which in fact proved to be the case.

Falkirk had been a severe blow to Scottish aspirations but it was by no means decisive.

Most of those who had died came from Galloway, the Borders and the Lothians and this still left huge reserves of rebellious men in the Highlands, in the North East, in the Lowlands and the Western Isles.

The country accepted an unstable triumvirate of Bishop William Lamberton of St. Andrews, Robert Bruce of Carrick and John Comyn the Red, Lord of Badenoch, as rulers but they regularly quarrelled and were replaced by various barons over the years while parliaments of lords met when necessary to try and bring order to the chaotic land.

While debates were going on in echoing chambers, William was busy attacking English supply trains and besieging Stirling Castle.

WILLIAM WALLACE FREEDOM FIGHTER

He ambushed convoys of English soldiers in woodlands and stole weapons and armour in sporadic raids.

He also appears to have been used as a diplomatic messenger to France by Bishop Lamberton. The latter schemed to make his country free while William relied more on physical might, being as pragmatic in this regard as Edward.

Along with five knights, William sailed to France, the country which had more sympathy with Scotland than with England, where Longshanks was as cordially hated and where the renown of the defiant Scots had raised their esteem to heroic levels.

William, who had sailed from Kirkcudbright to avoid English fleets, ran into pirate ships but the Scots more than held their own and took some of the pirates captive to France.

At Amiens William met with King Philip the Fair, a schemer as devious as Lamberton, although what took place remained secret behind closed doors.

Presumably they discussed how the Scots could best fight the English and how the French could help.

Tiring of inaction and keen to prove his credentials, William offered his sword and those of his companions in a campaign around the Bordeaux region where English knights had seized some land.

But Philip the Fair was playing an involved diplomatic and political game and aid to the Scots was not at this stage on his agenda and any overtures to him proved fruitless.

It suited him at the moment not to upset Edward so material aid to William was not forthcoming.

The Scottish envoy therefore returned home empty handed but in the years ahead was also used in diplomatic missions to Norway and Rome.

The latter visit to see Pope Boniface took place because the Pontiff was sympathetic to the Scottish cause and viewed the actions of the English as barbaric.

William's timely visit resulted in the Pope writing to Edward telling him that Scotland was a fief of the Holy See and had never belonged to the English sovereign who had no right to over-run it.

The Papal Bull was discussed at various conventions held by Edward and monastic orders were duly consulted but it was all a pompous show on the part of the English court which only responded because in that age religion was a reality in everyday and political affairs which could not be ignored.

The doctors of Civil Law at Oxford and Cambridge concocted a farrago of excuses for Edward's belligerence but all the so-called reasons were refuted in detail by Scottish ecclesiastics.

The basic point was that Edward could only take Scotland by conquest and his one entitlement to holding it was by force.

The Papal intrigues of William and Lamberton thus proved fruitless on a practical level where the English more or less did as they pleased but at least the Scots had proved in theological and ethical terms that they were in the right.

Undeterred by the imprecations of the Pope, Edward, rejuvenated in his sixties by a marriage to a young French princess, crossed the Solway in the Spring of 1300 on a rampaging expedition against Galloway where he clashed with the Red Comyn at Kirkcudbirght and took Caerlaverock Castle.

But although the green hills were dotted with the colourful tents containing the flower of English chivalry, the campaign, if such a title can be used to dignify the martial manoeuvrings, proved frustratingly inconclusive because the Scots refused to be drawn into a pitched battle, the memory of their humiliation at Falkirk being alarmingly fresh in the minds of the natives.

Over the next two years Edward mounted similar incursions into the Lowlands but, without a Wallace to lead them and with no support coming from abroad, the invaders found their opponents melting into the hills and woods.

Edward continued to view Scotland as an English province and even had the effrontery to draw up 'Ordinances for the Establishment of the Land of Scotland' which proposed a government of twenty Englishmen and ten elected representatives of the Scottish estates.

William, who had now returned from Rome, set up his makeshift headquarters in the wilds of Perthshire, a central point where he hoped to gather increasing forces. But he had only a ragged band of supporters at this time and could not defy the might of Edward's forces.

He did fight with English patrols and slew as many of the enemy as feasible.

He mounted a spirited attack against Dunkeld and massacred the garrison there before marching on Perth to which he laid siege.

Edward's forces pushed up as far north as Dunfermline where he wintered in late 1303, his armies creating havoc in their wake, burning villages, storming castles with their huge siege engines and stripping cathedrals in a scorched earth policy which even the king's subservient monastic supporters found difficult to justify.

His men destroyed the pride of Scottish cathedrals, Dunfermline Abbey, founded by St. Margaret in the 11th century, and a huge, rich source of religious ornament and piety which was reduced to a pile of rubble, an act of vandalism which the monkish chroniclers of the times described as "unscrupulous and vindictive".

The Scots eventually succeeded in obtaining a truce and various rebels were reprieved or mildly punished with exile.

This unusual lapse of mercy on Edward's part did not extend to William Wallace.

Longshanks had a bitter, unforgiving attitude to his old enemy and William was made aware that under no circumstances would he be shown any mercy whatsoever.

As if to emphasise this, Edward personally declared that he would hand over three hundred marks to the man who would bring him the head of the Wallace.

Seeing his country once more overwhelmed by the enemy, William retreated into his favourite fastnesses in the Selkirk Forest where he skulked and pondered his hazardous future.

Even in the unlikely event of a reprieve being offered to him, the thirst for freedom for himself and his country was now too deeply embedded in William's soul for his ever to contemplate bowing before the invaders.

Many of his former colleagues, tired and disheartened, bowed in submission to Edward in the hope that this would give them some peace and security but William never even contemplated such an action. He held out, determined to fight another day.

Edward and William were such implacable foes that the situation could only be resolved through the death of one of them.

CHAPTER TEN

DEATH AND TRANSFIGURATION

Wallace was now more or less on his own as a freedom fighter.

Edward had gradually worn down the opposition until there was hardly a spark of rebellion left in the Scottish countryside.

With a price on his head, a fugitive from the occupying forces, life was becoming increasingly dangerous for William. He had to rely on the loyalty of those who gave him shelter and sometimes on strangers.

The wildernesses of the countryside gave him some protection in which to hide but little in the way of comfort or encouragement.

And yet he seems to have given no thought of fleeing abroad. There was a long tradition of Scottish mercenaries fighting for European kingdoms and principalities and William himself had for a time fought under the banner of Philip the Fair of France. No doubt a man of William's physical stature and martial reputation would have been welcomed in many a Continental army but he stalwartly refused to quit the shores of his native land as if sensing that it was there that his destiny lay. He was so imbued with his sense of mission that he had decided to stand and fight for his cause or die in the process.

As the English tightened their grip on the countryside, Edward introduced a further refinement to his policy of hunting down the Wallace by stipulating that he would be extremely lenient and forgiving to any Scottish noble who had disgraced himself in the past by defying the English if they could just find it in themselves to bring him William dead or alive.

English officials backed by large bodies of troops now took over the running of the country and part of their duties involved hiring bounty hunters to track down William.

A network of spies and informers also made life more hazardous for William and his shrinking group of followers and areas in which he was believed to be sheltering were devastated with ruthless reprisals.

The capture of William had now become an obsession with Edward and he believed Scotland would never be pacified until the giant outlaw was destroyed.

A troop of cavalry under Sir Aymer de Valence chased William and his band the length of Stirlingshire in the midsummer of 1305 but the brigands escaped into the hills once again.

William wandered westwards and ominously into the realm of Sir John de Menteith, a slippery Scottish knight of Norman descent adept at changing sides, a former supporter of the Wallace cause when it was in the ascendant and now a quisling seeking to curry as much favour as possible from the English king.

WILLIAM WALLACE FREEDOM FIGHTER

De Menteith was Constable of Dumbarton in charge of Strathclyde and one of his spies told him that William was staying in a cottage at Robroyston in what is now north east Glasgow but what in those days was open countryside.

William was in bed with one of his girlfriends when de Menteith and sixty of his men surrounded the cottage around midnight.

As the alarm was raised, William leapt from his bed to find his sword had been stolen by a treacherous page. His most loyal follower was cut down as he stepped outside the door and William fought off the intruders with his bare hands.

A terrific scrap now ensued in the darkened confines of the cottage which only stopped when de Menteith shouted in that William would be taken to the safety of Dumbarton Castle and treated with respect and that, anyway, the cottage was surrounded by a large force of English knights (which was a lie) and resistance was therefore futile.

William naively allowed himself to be bound and led out where he realised he had been betrayed by the treacherous de Menteith.

While the latter was given an earldom by Edward, William, bound to a horse, was taken with a large, armed escort south to meet his awful fate at the hands of his vengeful foe who had planned his public punishment with fiendish precision.

The party surrounding the fettered giant travelled only at night and avoided areas where there might be support for William but once they were over the border the prisoner was displayed openly and mocked as he was led through towns and villages on the long, seventeen day journey to London, his only rest being in occasional dark, dank dungeons.

English propaganda had painted William as a monster and huge crowds gathered to gaze at him.

On Sunday August 22nd the party reached London and plans were put in hand for William's show trial, the result of which was a foregone conclusion.

There were reports that the surly giant was presented before his arch foe, King Edward, but no details of his confrontation have survived.

All accounts testify grudgingly to the dignity of the prisoner. Perhaps he realised this was the last act of his drama and he wanted to leave with an impression of calm, defiant courage which would further his cause as much as any military feat in the years ahead.

The proceedings now held were a backhanded compliment to William. All the panoply of state, church, court, chivalry and judiciary was assembled for the mock trial while the populace outside, whipped up by royal propaganda, bayed for his blood which they knew would be forthcoming soon.

On the clear, blue morning of Monday, August 23rd, 1305, William, erect, proud and still with a fierce, defiant glint in his savage eyes, was led, in chains on horseback and surrounded by a heavily armed escort, from his house of confinement in the parish of Fenchurch to the Great Hall of Westminster. Mayors, sheriffs and aldermen solemnly followed the procession.

A mocking laurel crown was placed on William's head, under other circumstances a sign of victory but put there by his jeering enemies to remind him of the boast made in the days of his triumphs that he would wear a crown in England's capital.

A commission of judges sat in their splendid red robes, supposedly to consider the case, in reality to rubberstamp the accused's execution.

The indictment which was read out was long and detailed and included sedition, homicide, robbery, arson, desecration and sacrilege and various other crimes.

There was no attempt to call witnesses, to produce evidence or to argue a case. William was not allowed to defend himself.

Nevertheless, at some point he became so angered at the charge of treason that he shouted out that he had never been a traitor to the King of England since he had never taken an oath of loyalty to him. This was patently the truth but was ignored by the court.

The other charges were tied up with William's long campaign against the English invaders and therefore came under the rules of war as opposed to the normal civilian criminal law.

Edward had committed worse atrocities and on a much grander scale than the Scots ever had and he had been the one to instigate the carnage yet he was now the accuser.

If ever there was a case of the victor rewriting history, this was it.

The farce was brought to a swift conclusion after the indictment was read out and the judges immediately gave their anonymous verdict of guilty.

Sir John de Segrave, the senior member of the court, then intoned, "That the said William, for the manifest sedition that he practised against the Lord King himself, by feloniously contriving and acting with a view to his death and to the abasement and subversion of his crown and royal dignity, by bearing a hostile banner against his liege lord in war to the death, shall be drawn from the Palace of Westminster to the Tower of London, and from the Tower to Aldgate, and so through the midst of the City to the Elms.

"And that for the robberies, homicides and felonies he committed in the realm of England and in the land of Scotland, he be there hanged, and afterwards taken down from the gallows. And that, inasmuch as he was an outlaw, and was not afterwards restored to the peace of the Lord King, he be decollated and decapitated.

"And that thereafter, for the measureless turpitude of his deeds towards God and Holy Church in burning down churches, with the vessels and litters wherein and whereon the body of Christ and the bodies of saints and other relics of these were placed, that the heart, the liver and lungs as well as all the other intestines of the said William, from which such perverted thoughts proceeded, be cast into the fire and burnt. And further, that inasmuch as it was not only against the Lord King himself, but against the whole Community of England and of Scotland, that he committed the aforesaid acts of sedition, spoliation, arson, and homicide, the body of the said William be cut up and divided into four parts, and that the head, so cut off, be set up on London Bridge, in the sight of such as pass by, whether by land or by water; and that one quarter be hung on a gibbet at Newcastle-upon-Tyne, another quarter at Berwick, a third quarter at Stirling , and the fourth at St. Johnston, as a warning and a deterrent to all that pass by and behold them."

The sentence was carried out at once.

Although hanging, drawing and quartering was a routine punishment for treason, the devious mind of Edward can be detected in some of the other refinements involved in this barbaric punishment.

William was carried from the Hall, stripped naked and

dragged behind two horses through the crowded streets for four miles. He was pelted with rubbish and hit with sticks all the way.

The parallel of the treatment of Jesus on Golgotha might have crossed William's mind since he asked the Archbishop of Canterbury who was present to hear his confession. He also asked that the book of psalms, which he carried everywhere with him and which of course contained his beloved, inspiring songs of David, be placed before him by a priest to give him comfort during his ordeal.

His hands bound, he was taken onto a wooden scaffold where he was partially hanged then cut down and revived so that he was conscious when he was castrated.

A gash was then made in his side and his intestines were pulled out and burned on a fire in front of his eyes.

The heart was then removed, finally thankfully inducing death, and displayed to the crowd.

Various other internal organs were removed and then the severed head was also displayed to the mob.

The scarlet torso was then chopped in four.

But even this barbaric procedure had not ended William's punishment.

Such was his reputation that it was decreed that his head be displayed on a pole at Westminster Bridge while his four limbs were ceremoniously conveyed to Newcastle, Berwick, Perth and Stirling, the scenes of his most successful exploits, and publicly displayed.

This martyrdom now made William immortal.

His conduct during his final ordeal inspired his countrymen and Edward, blinded by vengeful fury and with no advisors courageous enough to warn him of the long-term political dangers of the punishment he was inflicting, did not realise the resentment he was unleashing.

Thereafter, like King Arthur or Robin Hood, William's giant figure took on the epic proportions of a myth.

It was said his right arm, which hung over the sewers beside the bridge at Newcastle, contracted until a skeletal finger seemed to be pointing north to his native land as if warning the good burghers of northern England what to expect from the Scots.

The ghost of Wallace did not rest.

It haunted the tents of Robert the Bruce and his followers.

William's spirit was there as the Scottish nation gradually gathered to itself the confidence and strength to defy the English and eventually triumph.

It was there as the Scottish armies marched to glory and it was there to inspire during the darkest hours, stirring, restless and deep in the Caledonian psyche.

In time, statues and monuments were erected to William throughout Scotland.

These always depicted him as brave, huge, martial, resourceful, defiant and immensely strong and the legends of his martial qualities proved a tangible rallying point for his beleaguered countrymen.

Towns queued up to be associated with him and swords galore were found which were supposed to be his own special weapon.

For their part, the English failed to realise that the execution of the Wallace, far from being the end of an era, was in fact the beginning of a new one of bloodshed and revolt, ending with final victory for the Scottish nation.

Seven months after William's death Robert the Bruce had himself crowned King of Scotland at Scone and a couple of years later Edward died on the shores of the

Solway, still campaigning against those Scots he had so signally failed to subdue.

Longshanks had possessed the most astute military brain in Europe and had been in charge of the most efficient army. If these superbly led English cohorts, so formidably arrayed, could not subjugate their northern neighbours, there seemed little hope that Edward's successors would triumph.

His effeminate son was not of the same mettle whereas Robert the Bruce was more than capable of seizing the mantle of William Wallace and carrying on his good fight against the odds to the bitter or glorious end.

The English learned nothing from past mistakes and continued to treat the Scots prematurely as an already conquered people, with all the arrogance and contempt which that implies, and this suited the ambitions of Bruce who found ready support flocking to his banner.

William's example showed that brutal English might could be successfully defied - even after death - and in this he had truly worked out his destiny.

If William had scuttled abroad when things became too hot for him, dying on some foreign battlefield as a mere mercenary or ending his days an alcoholic wreck in some decadent Continental court, he would have been forgotten as a footnote in history, a wild rebel who promised much but in the end fled from the challenge.

But the fact that he stayed and fought on his native soil, even when all seemed lost and in fact was lost at that time, ensured his enshrinement as hero rather than transient outlaw.

Before his final capture, William's career was going nowhere fast. The circle was closing in on him and there seemed no way to break out afresh and create another Stirling Bridge.

DEATH AND TRANSFIGURATION

Only his martyrdom could have done that and Edward duly obliged and a few years later came Bannockburn when the English forces were comprehensively vanquished by the Scots and swept from the northern kingdom.

In a strange sense, William needed the stage of his terrible fate in London to act as a climax to his career.

Subconsciously, instinctively, he may even have been well aware of this, which might explain why he made no effort whatsoever to get out of the country, even on a temporary basis, and the bizarrely lax circumstances of his capture suggest he had been somewhat careless in looking after his personal safety at a time when he was in serious jeopardy from his marauding enemies who held the surrounding countryside in a tightening iron grip.

Perhaps William secretly welcomed the prospect of betrayal and martyrdom as a way of promoting his cause which at that point seemed irretrievably lost.

Perhaps he made himself a willing sacrificial victim on the altar of Scottish nationhood and independence.

It is difficult to appreciate anyone willingly submitting to such a ghastly fate but William may have foolishly thought he would be treated with some honour by his old foe and be given a dignified - and quick - death.

By the time he realised what was in store for him it would have been far too late to stage an escape.

Perhaps he too had been dazzled by Edward's pseudo-legality and pseudo-religiosity and believed the Plantagenet really was an honourable and pious monarch instead of the bitter, angry old hypocrite he in fact had become with a personal obsession about dominating the Scots in general and slaying William Wallace in particular.

The great thing about the Scottish patriot was his example. His excesses were ignored by his idolators and his prowess was enhanced by the minstrels and troubadours who spread his fame abroad and enshrined his exploits in vivid, poetic colours. Many a castle feast was enhanced with the martial tales of the Wallace and his adventures have remained colourful and thrilling right down to the present day with an epic, Hollywood film being dedicated to his tale.

William's achievement seems all the greater in retrospect when it is realised that in the stratified class structure of medieval, feudal Scotland he rose from nowhere with no material backing, no influential friends at court, no aristocratic lineage, no paid entourage, no immediate sycophants, no treasury, no personal financial backing, no dynastic claims to leadership, no previous military experience, no knowledge of how to wage a large-scale martial campaign, no support from abroad, no initial papal support, no way of judging the mood of the country or garnering support.

All William brought was his splendid personal gifts - his charisma, his driving energy, his fierce combativeness, his handsome appearance, his galvanising leadership qualities, his sense of his own destiny, his courage, his defiance, his burning patriotism, his faith in the common people, his belief in the eventual victory of his cause, his vision for the future nationhood of Scotland and his strategic planning.

It was quite a lot to pack into the thirty three years of his life.

He has left his countrymen a figure to look up to and an example of resolution against all the odds and he would have been well pleased with that.

The brief eight months of his reign as Guardian of

Scotland brought a touch of Camelot to Edinburgh where the best of the talents were gathered and encouraged, regardless of rank or connections. It was an example which was not forgotten by the Scottish people and it served as a blueprint for those in the future who believed they had their fingers on the pulse of the nation.

William Wallace is a hero the Scots can be well and truly proud of and it can only be hoped that figures of similar stature will appear in future if and when they are badly needed.